# A
# B
# SEE

**by Lucille Ogle and Tina Thoburn**
**Illustrated by Ralph Stobart**

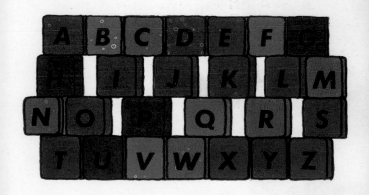

McGRAW-HILL BOOK COMPANY
New York   St. Louis   San Francisco   Düsseldorf
Johannesburg   Kuala Lumpur   London   Mexico
Montreal   New Delhi   Panama   Rio de Janeiro
Singapore   Sydney   Toronto

# ABOUT THIS BOOK

Two important first steps in learning to read, write, and spell are recognizing the letters of the alphabet and identifying the most common speech sounds related to them. A B SEE is designed to help your child take these first steps successfully.

In this book, both capital and lower case letters are presented in a variety of type and handwriting styles. Familiar objects whose names begin with the same sound are colorfully illustrated and grouped together under the letter or letters that spell that sound. The alphabetical arrangement of the book provides readiness for later understanding of the order of entries in dictionaries and other reference books. And, best of all, the letters and their sounds are related to the children's own names and favorite activities.

Written by Lucille Ogle and Tina Thoburn. Pictures by Ralph Stobart.

Printed in Japan.

Ogle, Lucille.
  A B see.
  SUMMARY: Introduces the letters of the alphabet and the most common speech sounds related to each letter.
  1. English language—Study and teaching (Primary)—Juvenile literature. [1. Alphabet books]
I. Thoburn, Tina, joint author.   II. Stobart, Ralph, illus.   III. Title.
LB1528.034   1973        372.4'145   [E]        73-3423
ISBN 0-07-047497-4
ISBN 0-07-047498-2 (lib. bdg.)

# HOW TO USE *A B SEE*

First, let your child get acquainted with the book and learn the names of the objects pictured in it. Talk about the dressed-up children and what they are doing.

When he begins to show curiosity about the letters, help him learn their names and sounds. This is a longterm process, so move slowly and "play" with one letter/sound combination at a time. (Some letters such as *a, c,* and *g* have more than one letter to spell them, e.g., *sh, ch,* and *wh.*) You may introduce the letters in alphabetical order or you may jump around. Children often like to start with the letters in their own names. To teach *D,* for example, start on page 24. After your child identifies the occupation of the boy in the picture, point to the word beneath it and say that *doctor* begins with *d.* Show the capital (big) *D* and lower case (little) *d* at the top of page 25. Read the sentences and talk about the other ways *d* can look. Turn to page 26. Ask your child if he can find any *d*'s there. Read the sentence at the top and say the *d* words together, slightly exaggerating the beginning sound. Continue on to page 27, ending with the silly verse at the bottom.

Between sessions with the book, play alphabet and letter/sound games with your child. Have him identify letters in newspapers, on signs, and so on. Show him how to write them (models are provided in the book). Sing alphabet songs that stress the order of letters. And have him give other words that begin with the same sound as one you name. More A B SEE games may be found on pages 124 and 125.

astronaut

# Aa

This is the letter A.

It can be printed in many different sizes and shapes.

This is how A looks when we write it.

# A
## a

A usually has the sound
of A in Andrew and Anne.

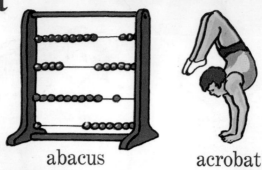

abacus

acrobat

alligator

| A | B | C | D | E | F | G |
| H | I | J | K | L | M |
| N | O | P | Q | R | S |
| T | U | V | W | X | Y | Z |

alphabet

ambulance

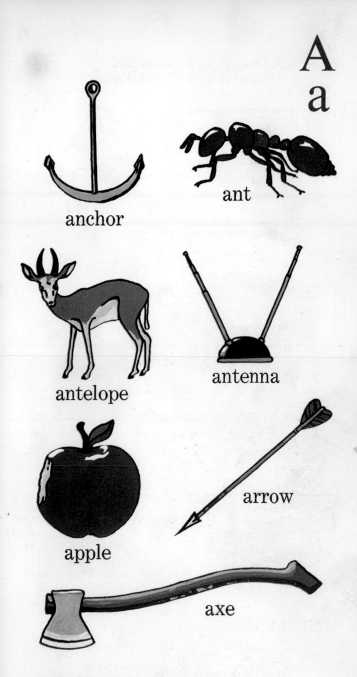

# A a

anchor

ant

antelope

antenna

apple

arrow

axe

Ali Baba, Ali Kazaam,
Ask your aunt for bread and jam.

11

# A
## a

Sometimes **A** has the sound of **A** in **Amy** and **Abraham**.

acorn

angel

angelfish

ape

apron

aviator

April, April, what have you made?
Angel food cake and lemonade.

A and r together
sound like **Ar** in **Ar**thur.

# AR
ar

arch

ark

armadillo

armor

artist

Arny Carny, sound the al**ar**m!
An **aar**dvark's lost on **Ar**len's f**ar**m.

ballerina

# Bb

This is the letter B.

It can be printed in many different sizes and shapes.

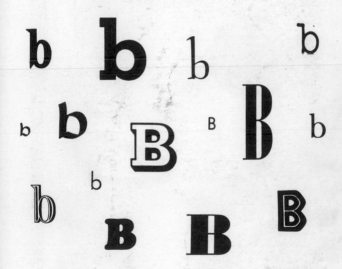

This is how B looks when we write it.

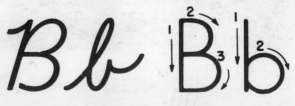

# B
# b

B has a bubbly sound
in **Betty** and **Bob** and **Bill**.

baby

ball

balloon

banana

beads

beans

bear

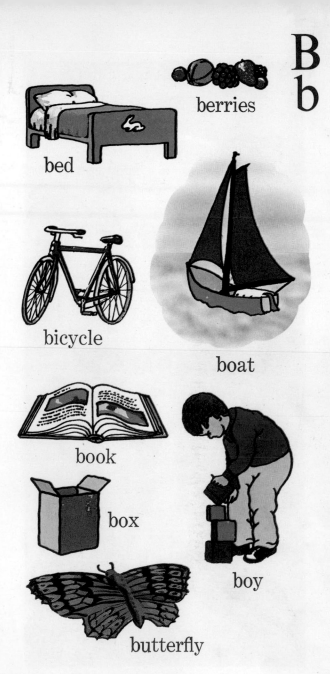

**B b**

berries

bed

bicycle

boat

book

box

boy

butterfly

Buzzy, buzzy bumblebees,
Busy buzzing on the breeze.

cowboy

18

This is the letter C.

It can be printed in many
different sizes and shapes.

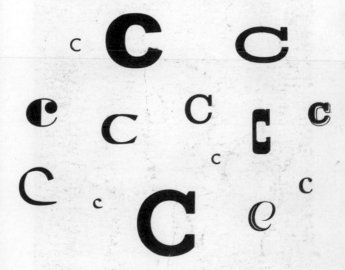

This is how C looks
when we write it.

# C
# c

C has a hard sound
in Caroline and Carl.

cake

camel

candle

canoe

car

cat

cards

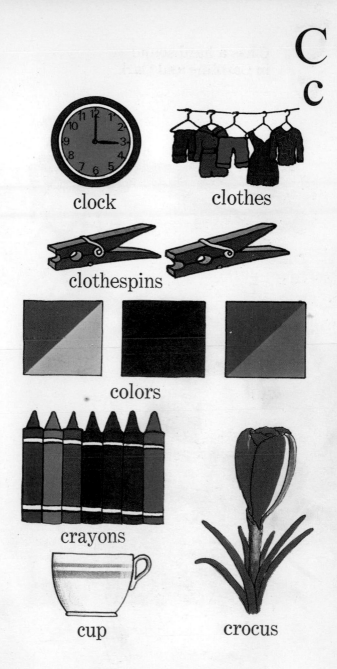

clock

clothes

clothespins

colors

crayons

cup

crocus

How many cans can a canner can
If a canner can can cans?

21

# C
# c

C has a soft sound
in Cecil and Cecile.

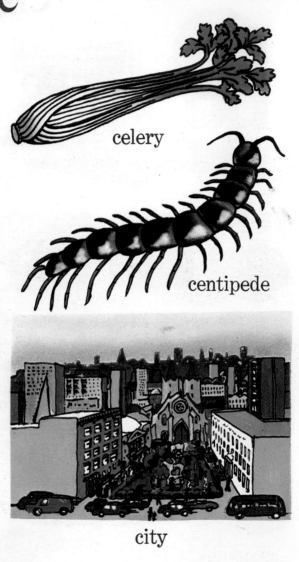

celery

centipede

city

Circle, circle, circle all around.
Cindy in the center, touch the ground.

C and h together
sound like the **Ch** in Charles.

# CH
## ch

chair

cheese

cherries

chicken

chicks

chipmunk

church

Children here, children there,
Charming children everywhere.

23

doctor

# Dd

This is the letter D.

It can be printed in many different sizes and shapes.

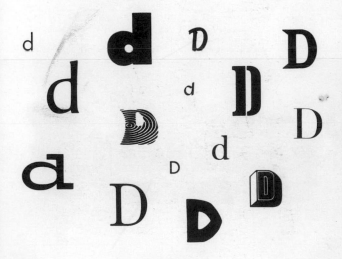

This is how D looks when we write it.

# D
# d

D sounds like the D
in Dorothy and Dick.

darts

desk

dinosaur

dog

dishes

# D d

doll

dolphin

dominoes

donkey

drum

duck

Diane's daughter is Donald's cousin.
She dunks doughnuts by the dozen.

27

engineer

# Ee

This is the letter E.

It can be printed in many different sizes and shapes.

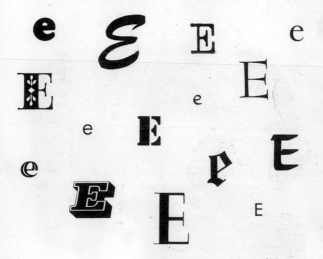

This is how E looks when we write it.

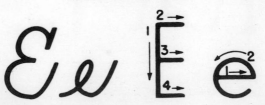

# E e

The **E** in **Edward** has a short **E** sound.

elephant

egg

elf

Eskimo

elk

Did you ever see an elephant on an escalator?

The **E** in **Edith**
has a long **E** sound.

# E
## e

eagle

easel

eel

egret

eland

emu

"**Eeeee**k, **Eeeee**k, **E**ek,"
The mouse did squ**e**ak.

fireman

32

# Ff

This is the letter F.

It can be printed in many different sizes and shapes.

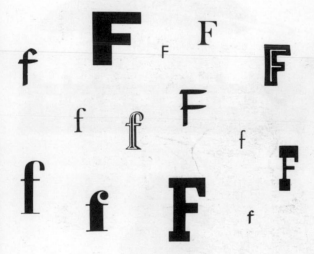

This is how F looks when we write it.

# F
## f

F sounds like the F
in Felicia and Fred.

fan

farmer

feather

fence

fire

fig

fireplace

# F
# f

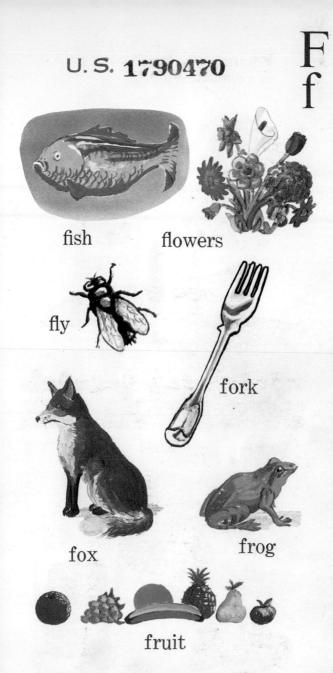

fish

flowers

fly

fork

fox

frog

fruit

I helped my father fix the fan;
He says I am his fix-it man.

35

gardener

# Gg

This is the letter G.

It can be printed in many different sizes and shapes.

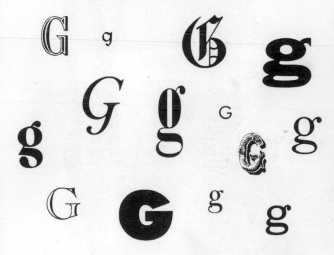

This is how G looks when we write it.

# G
# g

G has a good hard sound
in Gary and Goliath.

garage

garden

gate

ghost

girl

# G g

glove

goat

goldfish

goose

gosling

grapefruit

grapes

grasshopper

Gertrude giggled and giggled.
Guess why?

39

# G
g

G has a gentle sound
in Geraldine and George.

geranium

gerbil

giant

# G g

gingerbread

giraffe

gypsy

Ginger cookies, ginger fizz,
I like the sound of "gee whizz!"

hairdresser

# Hh

This is the letter H.

It can be printed in many different sizes and shapes.

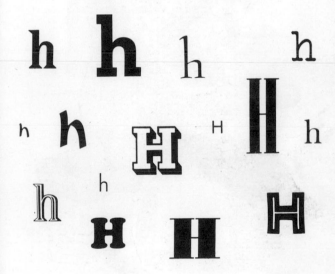

This is how H looks when we write it.

# H h

Hear the sound of H in Holly and Howard?

hairbrush

ham

hammer

handkerchief

harmonica

hat

helicopter

hen

44

# H h

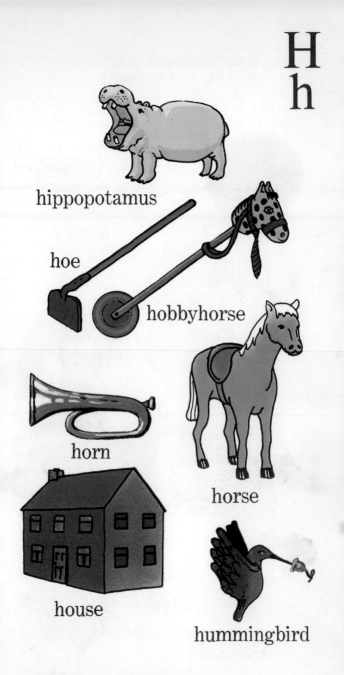

hippopotamus

hoe

hobbyhorse

horn

horse

house

hummingbird

Hippity hop, hippity hop,
Hop and hop, and never stop.

45

ice skater

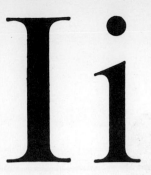

This is the letter I.

It can be printed in many different sizes and shapes.

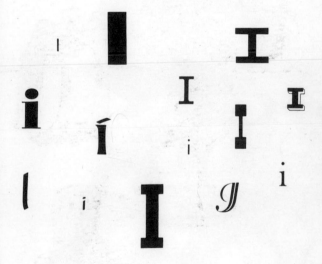

This is how I looks when we write it.

47

# I i

The short I sounds
like the I in Isadore.

igloo

iguana

inchworm

impala

If Isabelle is an imp,
Then an imp is Isabelle.

Here is long I, which sounds like the I in Irene.

# I i

ibis

ice cream

ice skates

icicles

iris

iron

ivy

I scream, you scream,
We all scream for ice cream.

juggler

This is the letter J.

It can be printed in many
different sizes and shapes.

This is how J looks
when we write it.

51

# J
# j

Just pronounce J
like the J in **Jane**.

jack-in-the-box    jack-o'-lantern

jacks

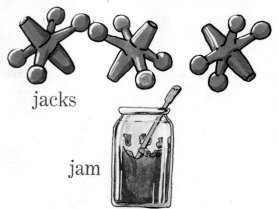

jam

jaguar

52

J j

jet

jewels

jug

jumping jack

Jig and jog and jump for joy,
Join the group, each girl and boy.

king

# Kk

This is the letter K.

It can be printed in many different sizes and shapes.

This is how K looks when we write it.

# K
## k

Sound K like the sound
of K in Kathleen.

kangaroo

kayak

kennel

key

kettle

I'm the king of the castle
and the keeper of the keys.

# K k

kid      kite

kitten      koala

Sometimes K doesn't seem
to have any sound at all.

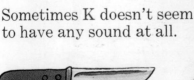

knife

knot

knight

Knock, knock, who's there?
I don't know and I don't care.

57

librarian

# L1

This is the letter L.

It can be printed in many different sizes and shapes.

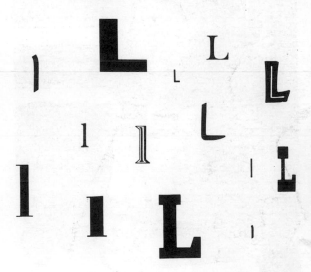

This is how L looks when we write it.

# L
# l

Listen to the sound of L
in Lillie and Larry and Lee.

ladybug

lamb

lamp

lantern

leaf

lemon

L l

leopard

lettuce

lighthouse

lizard

lobster

lollipop

log

Lil, Lil, can't sit still,
She chased a billy goat over the hill.

mechanic

# Mm

This is the letter M.

It can be printed in many different sizes and shapes.

This is how M looks when we write it.

# M
# m

Make the merry sound of M as the sound of M in Mark.

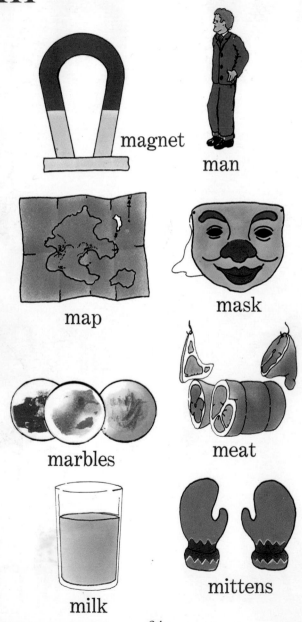

magnet

man

map

mask

marbles

meat

milk

mittens

64

# M
## m

monkey

moon

moose

motorcycle

mushroom

mouse

mountain

We're mixing muffins, Mother and me.
We'll have them with milk for
afternoon tea.

nurse

# Nn

This is the letter N.

It can be printed in many different sizes and shapes.

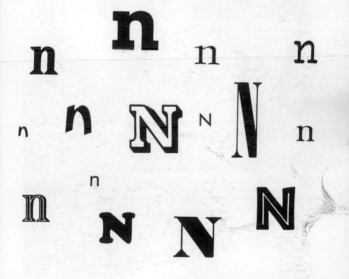

This is how N looks when we write it.

# N n

N sounds like the N
in Neal and Nancy.

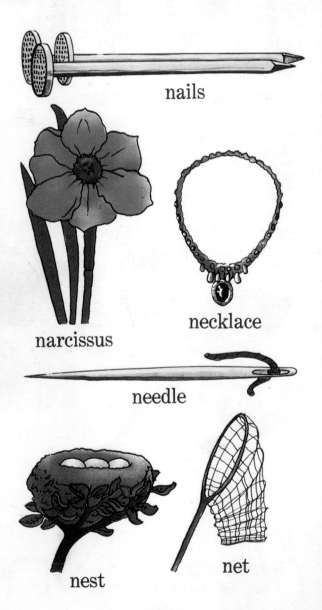

nails

narcissus

necklace

needle

nest

net

# N n

newspaper

nightgown

notebook

numbers

nuthatch

nuts

Engine, engine, Number Nine,
Running on the Northern line.

# oceanographer

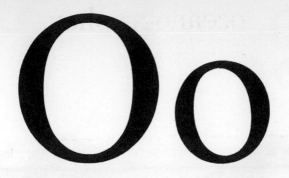

This is the letter O.

It can be printed in many different sizes and shapes.

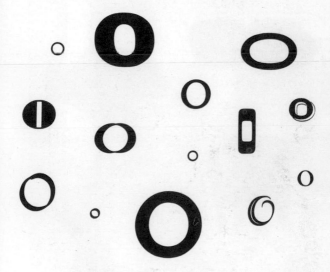

This is how O looks when we write it.

# O
# O

Short O sounds
like the O in Oscar.

ocelot

octopus

olives

ostrich

ox

otter

Og, bog,
A big fat hog.

# O o

Long O sounds like the O in opal.

oak leaf

okra

oboe

oval

overalls

overcoat

Oh, oh, Daddy-o,
This old boat just won't go!

policeman

# Pp

This is the letter P.

It can be printed in many different sizes and shapes.

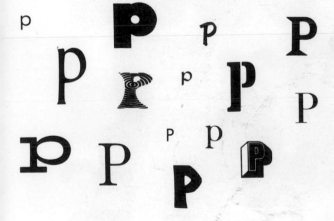

This is how P looks when we write it.

# P
# p

Please pronounce P
like the P in Paul.

pail

pan

paints

panda

pansy

parachute

parrot

# P p

peach

peanuts

pear

pegs

pen

pencil

penguin

pig

Peter Piper picked a peck
of pickled peppers.

77

queen

# Qq

This is the letter Q.

It can be printed in many different sizes and shapes.

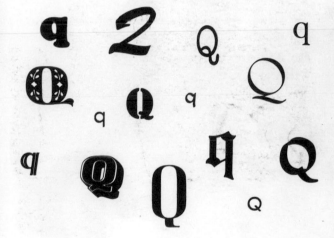

This is how Q looks when we write it.

# Q q

Quickly say **Q**
the way it sounds in **Quinby**.

quahog

quail

quartet

Queen Anne's lace

question mark

80

# Q q

quetzal

quilt

quince

quintuplets

Quentin Quiggly
quit quite quickly.

ringmaster

# Rr

This is the letter R.

It can be printed in many different sizes and shapes.

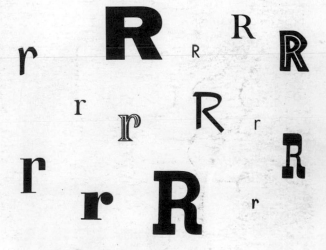

This is how R looks when we write it.

# R
# r

R has a ringing sound
in Ruth and Rachel and Ron.

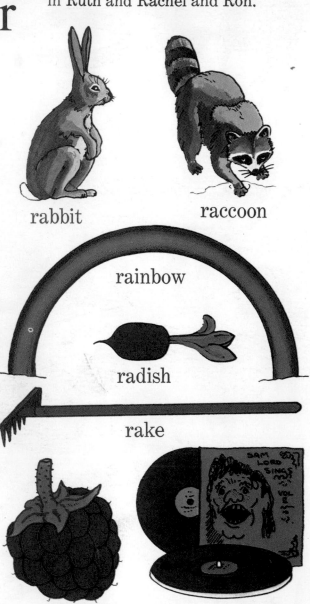

rabbit

raccoon

rainbow

radish

rake

raspberry

records

# R r

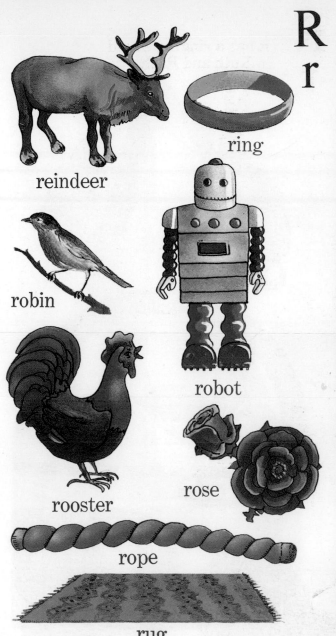

reindeer

ring

robin

robot

rooster

rose

rope

rug

Round and round the rugged rock
The ragged rascal ran.

85

sailor

# Ss

This is the letter S.

It can be printed in many
different sizes and shapes.

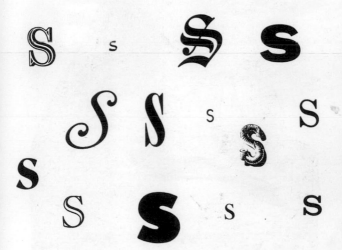

This is how S looks
when we write it.

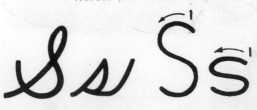

# S
## s

Say S so it sounds
like S in **Sally** and **Sam.**

sailboat

salad

sandpiper

satellite

saw

school

scissors

screwdriver

**S** **s**

seal

scooter

sled

skates

snake

snowflake

snowman

soap

89

# S
## s

soup

squirrel

starfish

stool

strawberry

submarine

sun

swing

Sing a silly seesaw song:
Sandbox full of salt.

# SH
## sh

S and h together
sound like the Sh in Sheila.

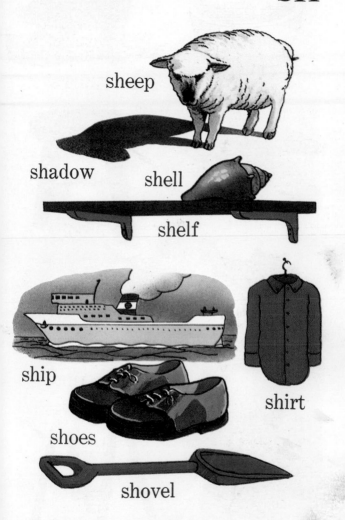

sheep

shadow

shell

shelf

ship

shirt

shoes

shovel

She sells seashells
by the seashore.

teacher

# T t

This is the letter T.

It can be printed in many different sizes and shapes.

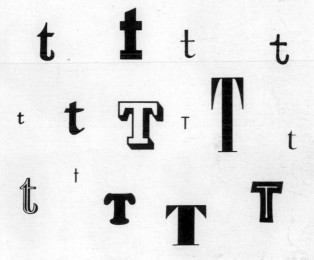

This is how T looks when we write it.

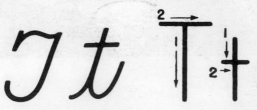

# T
## t

Take time to say **T**
as in Terry and Tom.

table

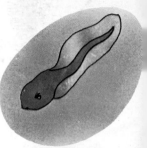
tadpole

tambourine

teapot

telephone

television

tent

tiger

94

tomato

tools

top

toucan

tractor

train

tree

tricycle

Twist and turn, count to ten;
Tumble down, then start again.

# T t

triplets

truck

tugboat

tulip

turkey

turtle

twins

T and h together often sound like the Th in Thelma.

thank-you note

thermometer

thermos

thimble

thread

thrush

Theophilus thrust three thousand thistles through the thick of his thumb.

unicyclist

# Uu

This is the letter U.

It can be printed in many different sizes and shapes.

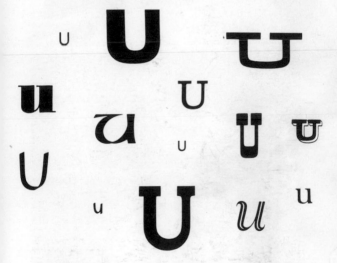

This is how U looks when we write it.

# U
## u

U has a short sound
in Umberto.

umbrella

umbrella bird

umpire

underwear

Up and over, down and under,
See the lightning chase the thunder.

# U u

U says its own name U
in Una.

ukulele

unicorn

unicycle

United States

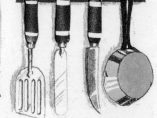

United Nations

utensils

"Utensils are useful," the unicorn said,
"But I open cans with the horn
on my head."

violinist

This is the letter V.

It can be printed in many
different sizes and shapes.

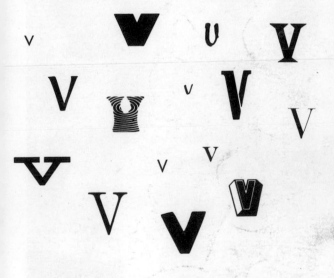

This is how V looks
when we write it.

# V
# V

vacuum

valentine

vase

vegetables

vicuña

village

vine

104

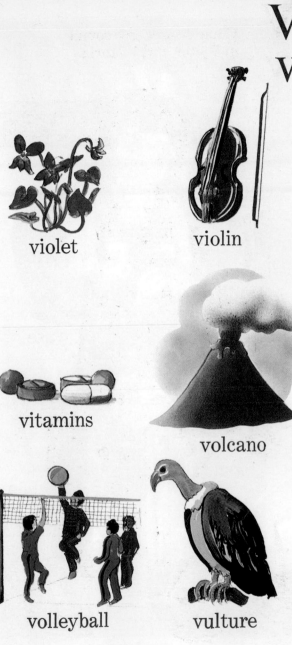

V v

violet

violin

vitamins

volcano

volleyball

vulture

Violets on a valentine
Say, "Love me, I am ever thine."

waitress

# Ww

This is the letter W.

It can be printed in many different sizes and shapes.

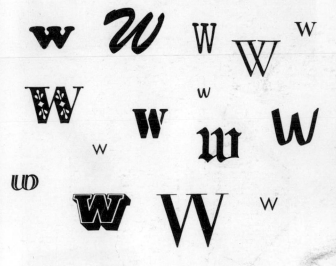

This is how W looks when we write it.

# W
# W

W has a wonderful sound
in Walter and Wendy and Wu.

waffle

wagon

wall

walrus

wand

wasp

watch

waterfall

# W
## W

water lily

windmill

window

wishbone

witch

wolf

woodpecker

worm

Will you, won't you,
Will you, won't you,
Will you waltz with me?

# WH
## wh

When w and h are together they sound like the wh in why.

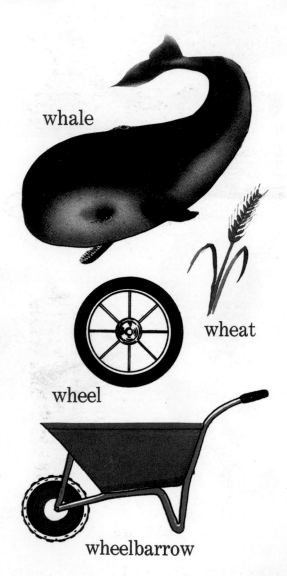

whale

wheat

wheel

wheelbarrow

110

# WH
# wh

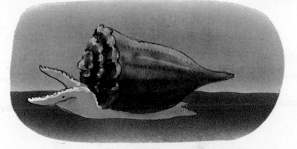

whelk

whip

whirligig

whistle

whiskers

Whether it rains or whether it snows,
We shall have weather, whether or no.

xylophonist

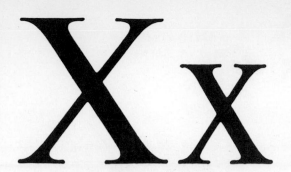

This is the letter X.

It can be printed in many
different sizes and shapes.

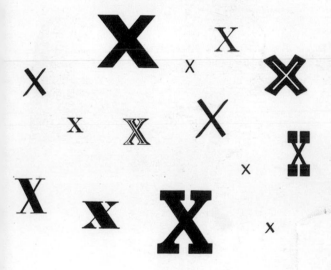

This is how X looks
when we write it.

# X
### X

X is extra special;
Hear it in Xerxes.

xebec

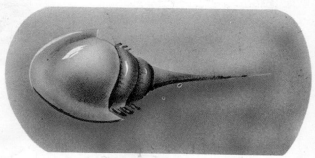

xiposuran

xylophone

Hear the X at the end
of these words?

X
x

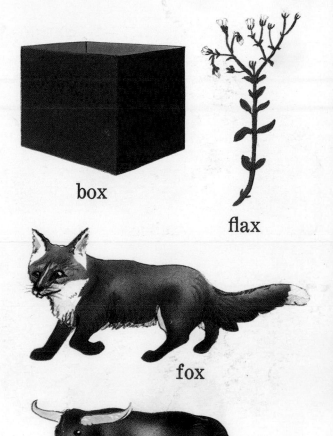

box

flax

fox

ox

We send you kisses.
X X X X X X X X X X X X X

115

# yachtsman

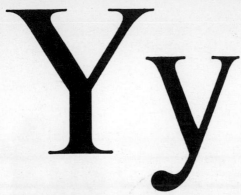

This is the letter Y.

It can be printed in many
different sizes and shapes.

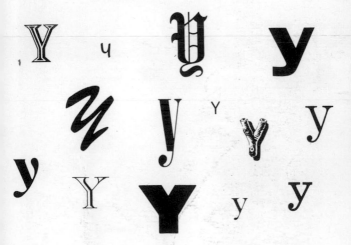

This is how Y looks
when we write it.

117

# Y
# y

You can hear the sound of y
at the beginning of Yolanda.

yacht

yak

yam

yard

yarn

yarrow

yawl

# Y y

year

yellowtail

yoke

yoyo

yucca

Yip-i-yaddy-i-yay, i-yay,
Yip-i-yaddy-i-yay!

119

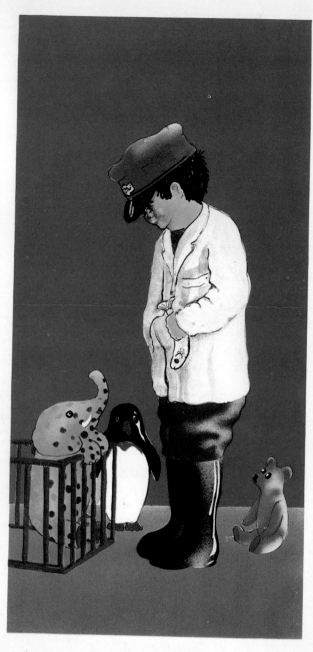

zoo keeper

# Zz

This is the letter Z.

It can be printed in many
different sizes and shapes.

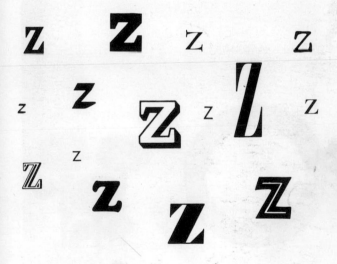

This is how Z looks
when we write it.

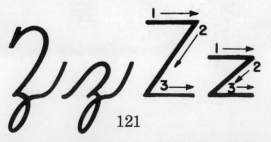

# Z
## Z

Z has a zizzy sound
In **Z**elda and **Z**ack and **Z**oe.

zebra

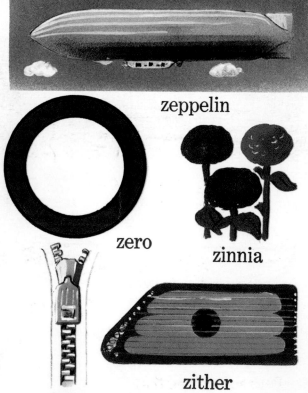

zeppelin

zero

zinnia

zipper

zither

zigzag

zoo

zucchini

zyzzyva

Bees say z when they
buzzzz zzzz zzzz zzzz.

# More *A B See* Games

**1.** Have your child help you make some alphabet cards. Cut out fifty-two squares of cardboard—2″ x 2″ is a good size. On one side of each card write a capital letter and on the other side write the corresponding lower-case letter. Draw a line across the very bottom of each card as a clue to which side up the letter must be placed to be correct. Use four different colors of crayon or marking pen so that when you have finished you have four complete alphabets, one of each color. For example, you might have red capital letters backed by blue lower-case letters, and green capital letters backed by yellow lower-case letters.

It is not necessary to make all the cards at one time. For younger children it will be more instructive to complete one letter (two cards) at a time, talking about it as you cut and write. Compare the letter forms with those in *A B See.*

**2.** Use the alphabet cards in these three matching games:

a. Scatter the cards on a table or on the floor. Have your child turn them so that all capital letters are facing up and the line is at the bottom of the card. Pick up one of the cards, for example, the red *E*. Say, "I have an *E*. Can you find another *E*?" He must find the blue *E*, name it, and hold it next to yours to show that it matches. Continue in this way until all the capital letters have been matched.

b. Follow the same procedure, but this time have the lower-case letters named and matched.

c. Use one set of capital letters and one set of lower-case letters, for example, the red and yellow ones. Pick up a capital letter, name it, and ask your child to find the lower-case letter with the same name.

This is a very much harder task than the previous two, so give your child time to check his choice by turning the card over and comparing capital letters before making his final decision. As he becomes more familiar with the letter pairs, he will need to do less checking.

**3.** After your child has learned to recognize and name many of the individual letters, help him learn to put them in alphabetical order. (This in turn will help him learn to recognize and name the other letters.) First use a set of alphabet cards with all capital letters. After they have been arranged in A-B-C order, each can be turned over to show the a-b-c order of

124

lower-case letters. Later have your child begin with lower-case letters and reverse the process. Still later, some children will enjoy arranging the letters in order regardless of the form, for example, A-b-C-d-e and so on.

4. The traditional game of Grandmother's Trunk is lots of fun for the whole family, and it helps children learn to distinguish the beginning sounds of words. Someone starts by saying, "Grandmother is going on a trip. She is packing her trunk and in it she will put a hat." The word "hat" is a clue that all the other things Grandmother packs for this vacation must begin with the *h* sound. Each player in turn repeats the two sentences and adds another item, for example, "... her hat and a horn." Grandmother is a rare character—she may also take along a house, hip boots, or a hippopotamus!

5. Another enjoyable game that stresses beginning sounds is a variation of I Spy. For example, say, "I see something in this room that begins the same as 'Walter.'" The other players must guess such things as wall, watch, or window until they guess the object you were thinking about. The one who guesses correctly may have the next turn to be the spy.

6. After your child has learned to associate the letters with the beginning sounds of words pictured in *A B See,* name objects around the house and have him pick out the alphabet card that shows how the word begins. Start with some of the regular letters, such as *b, d, m,* and *r,* then move on to those that have different sounds.

7. Show your child how to use his alphabet cards to spell words. Start with his own name, then have him copy words that appear in *A B See.* Be sure that he puts the beginning letter of the word at the left and proceeds in order toward the right. Have him name the letters, then read the complete word.